HILLBILLY COOKIN

By The Tates

BISCUIT AND CORN MEAL MAKINS

Howdy Folks. We-uns are proud you furriners come to see us right along. Maybe we figger you-uns must sort of like us, and some real purty good fishing places. And we shore hope you like our eatin. Some of it's powerful rib ticklin. We put in some recipes for you-uns to try special. There's also some maybe you'd just like to know about.

When our grandpappies and grandmas had to settle matters with Indians, bars and British, they had to live off what the land had to offer. Hard work meant a big appetite and wimmen folks had to sort of mix ways of cooking they learnt back home with what they could find in the wilderness. And they did powerful well.

That's why we put together this cookbook. We hope you like it.

★   ★   ★

When we git up early and see the east turn orangelike over the mountain tops afore the sun cuts the mist in the purty valleys, you kind of forgit aches and pains and morning chill. In your heart you just plain know God is in his place in spite of some men. Wild things know that, just as they know for every good summer, winter must growl a-crost mountans to our west and drive us to our hearths as the world outdoors puts on its bed sheet of snow. And like the Good Book says, I feel strong when I can look upon the hills from which comes strength.

★   ★   ★

All recipes wrote in citified style.

BISCUITS

Biscuits is good fur soppin, puttin under your gravy or syrup and with all main dishes. Lightbread is always good eatin. But corn meal pushes flour for the many ways you can use it to feed a hungry stomach. Indians depended on corn, and if the first settlers hadn't learnt how good corn was, they wouldn't have made it so well.

★   ★   ★

SOUR MILK BISCUITS

2 cups flour
1 teaspoon baking powder
¾ teaspoon salt
1/3 teaspoon soda
4 teaspoons fat
2/3 cups buttermilk

Mix dry, then cut in fat with two knives. Add milk and knead lightly. Roll and cut. Bake at from 450 to 500.

★   ★   ★

BEATEN BISCUITS

Company is always honored when you fix these up. Like teacake, they ain't meant to fill you up like regular biscuits. But they shore taste good.

RECIPE

1½ lbs plain flour
1½ teaspoon salt
1 tablespoon sugar
6 ounces fat
1 cup cold water.

Sift dry ingredients then cut in fat; mix into stiff dough. Knead smooth when start beating. Use wood beater and keep going till dough is light and velvety. Use small cutter. Take fork and prick dough, just on top. Bake for half hour at 350, then down to 325 another half hour. Now cut to 225 degrees for another half hour. If you ain't sure, shake the pan. If the biscuits rattle, they're done. Don't let them start to brown.

4

SPOON CORNBREAD

We used to look forward to Sunday dinners when they had this.

RECIPE

2 cups water   1 tablespoon butter
1 cup milk   2 eggs
1 cup cornmeal   2 teaspoons salt

Mix water and meal. Bring slowly up to the boiling point and cook five minutes. Add well beaten eggs and other ingredients. Beat thoroughly and pour into a well greased pan. Bake 25 minutes in hot oven.

★　　　★　　　★

HUSH PUPPIES

These little rascals give the right tang when you got a mess of fish all ready to eat.

RECIPE

1 egg   1 pint white cornmeal
1 pint thick buttermilk   1 teaspoon salt
1 teaspoon soda   1 tablespoon fat
2 small or one big onion, chopped fine

Heat the oven to 500 F. and place the bread pan in the oven to heat. Beat the egg slightly and add the remaining ingredients. Stir well. Grease the pan. Drop the mixture from a big spoon and cook 20 minutes at 400 degrees.

If you like open fire cooking, let your fat barely cover pan or skillet and drop in mixture. Cover pan. Watch to keep from overcooking.

★　　　★　　　★

CORN STICKS AND MUFFINS

Leave out onion and make otherwise as you would hush puppies. Mould and bake in oven 20 minutes.

★　　　★　　　★

A whistling girl and a crowing hen will always come to some bad end.

MR. WALKER'S GRATED CORN MUFFINS

Maybe Mr. Walker learnt this recipe from settlers who knowed about Indian ways of cookin.

RECIPE

When roasting ears get too hard to fry, shuck as many as needed. Use a coarse grater to get kernels off cob. To make up a bait of batter, use 1 cup cornmeal to each 2 ears of corn. Add 1 teaspoon soda and 1 teaspoon salt. Pour in just enough water to keep batter stiff enough to pour slowly. Grease muffin rings well and have them hot before putting in butter. Cook real fast and add butter to muffins while they're hot.

★　　★　　★

HASHED HOMINY

This goes fine with sausage or kraut, or both.

RECIPE

2 cups strained hominy
4 well beaten eggs

Butter as needed
Salt and pepper seasoning.

Brown hominy in skillet over medium heat. Use about 1 tablespoon butter or cooking oil. Put in beaten eggs with hominy. Season, then stir. When hominy gets brown look, remove and serve.

★　　★　　★

JUST PLAIN MUSH

Makin cornmeal mush ain't a problem a-tall. I've seen Aunt Liza stand afore a kettle with a pan of meal and a wooden spoon. With her left hand she'd put in salted meal and with her right she'd stir the mixture, and afore you could say scat you had mush.

Have the water in the kettle boiling hot. Put in a tablespoon salt. Start with a half gallon water. Put in a handful of meal, stir with spoon or stick, pour in more meal and stir again. Takes around a half hour after you got what you consider the right thickness. Usually, the puffing up tells you when it's just about done.

For serving, hot or cold, add milk or butter and more salt, if you like it that way. Or you can sweeten, or use gravy.

HOE CAKES

As fur as we can learn, hoe cakes was the beginnin of hot bread with early settlers. They was cooked in fireplaces and even on hot coals afore stoves were hauled in.

RECIPE

2 cups cornmeal
½ teaspoon salt
2 tablespoons bacon fat or

other shortening
1 cup hot water
1½ cup cold water

Mix salt in meal, then pour hot water on the mix, add enough cold water to thin the mush till it will pour sort of slow out of the bowl. Add melted fat. Drop batter by spoonfulls on a hot griddle or skillet. Turn till both sides are brown.

★ ★ ★

CORN PONE

Fancier than hoe cakes but tastier to most folks.

RECIPE

2½ cups cornmeal
1½ cups boiling water
½ cup bacon drippings
1 cup buttermilk
½ cup cold water

½ teaspoon soda
2 eggs
1 cup flour
2 teaspoons baking powder
1 teaspoon salt

Pour boiling water over meal in bowl. Add bacon drippings, cool, then stir in buttermilk and cold water. Next add beaten eggs and flour, baking powder, soda and salt, all sifted together first. Beat thoroughly, turn into a well greased hot pan, with the batter a half inch deep. Bake in moderate oven 25 minutes.

★ ★ ★

CRACKLIN BREAD

We always enjoyed this at hog killing time.

2 cups cornmeal
1 tablespoon salt
1 cup cracklins

Enough hot water to make into dough thick enough to shape into small loaves. It's better to use cracklins with the least fat, and be sure to break them into small pieces. Bake in a moderate oven—400 to 450 degrees for around 45 minutes.

CORN LIGHTBREAD (2 loaves)

Here's a taste fetcher that's good, hot or cold.

RECIPE

Moisten 2 cups waterground meal with cold water. Add 2 cups boiling water and let rise overnight in a warm place. Add 1 cup buttermilk, 1 teaspoon soda, 1 tablespoon salt, 1 cup sugar, 1 cup flour, 1 pint warm water and 1 quart meal to make a batter which will streak the spoon. Let rise 1 to 1½ hours. Bake in a greased pan 1 hour at 375 degrees. Cover and leave 24 hours.

★   ★   ★

STEAMED CORNBREAD

This is for folks who like a little sweetening for a change.

RECIPE

4 cups meal	1 cup white flour
3 cups buttermilk	2 teaspoons salt
2 teaspoons soda	1 cup molasses

Cook like brown bread.

★   ★   ★

MORE ABOUT MUSH

I reckon mush was the first cereal dish in these parts. Maw would take stone ground corn meal and pour water on it from a steaming kettle, and when it thickened on a slow fire, it was mush, ready to eat with salt and butter, cream and sugar, or how you want it. Maw would take the leftover and fry patties in grease.

★   ★   ★

If you're drivin where the mark of old furrows show on hillsides now turned to grass, you shorely must have wondered how they farmed so steep. Well, it was done with a hillside plow. The way it worked, a feller plowed to one end of the field, turned his plow around and swung the point, mounted on a swivel, so's it would turn dirt the other way.

8

MUSH BISCUITS

1 quart mush
1 cake yeast
1 cup potato water
1 cup lard
1 cup sugar
a dab of salt
2/3 cup flour

Dissolve yeast in warm water, mix ingredients, add yeast and stir in flour, enough to make stiff dough. Set to rise where it's warm. When dough rises twice its size, roll out and cut into biscuits. Bake as you would flour biscuits.

★　　★　　★

HOMINY AND GRITS

We-uns who are old, recollect the ash hopper filled with wood ashes. When water was run through the hopper, you got strong lye, which was powerful useful. You made lye soap and hominy with the yeller water. Hominy was made by soaking dried corn in lye water till the skin peeled off and was ready for boilin. Grits is hominy grains busted up. Next time you see canned hominy or boxed grits, remember how it used to be made.

★　　★　　★

SWEET CORN PUDDIN

This goes fine with any main dish.

RECIPE

10 or 12 ears corn
1½ tablespoon sugar
1 quart whole milk
Salt to taste
2 tablespoons flour
1 tablesspoon butter
3 eggs

Grate corn and mix with milk. To make smoother, run through colander. Work flour and butter creamy, then beat in sugar and egg yolks. Add beaten whites. Put into corn and milk mix and salt to taste. Bake. If you want it sweeter, add sugar and cream.

★　　★　　★

Killin frosts are over when oak leaves are longer'n and inch.

EGG BREAD

In a way I reckon you-uns can regard this recipe as the backbone of cornmeal eatin. Egg bread goes with all main dishes.

RECIPE

2½ cups cornmeal	½ teaspoon soda
1½ cups boiling water	2 eggs
½ cup bacon drippings	1 cup flour
1 cup buttermilk	2 teaspoons baking soda
½ cup cold water	1 teaspoon salt

Pour boiling water over cornmeal in a bowl. Add bacon drippings and cool, then stir in buttermilk and cold water. Next add well beaten eggs, flour, baking powder, soda and salt sifted together. Beat thoroughly. Turn into a well greased, smoking hot baking pan, with the batter a half inch deep. Bake in a moderate oven 20 to 25 degrees. Cut into squares.

★ ★ ★

MUSH BUSCUITS

1 quart hot water	1 cup lard
Corn meal	1 cup sugar
1 cake yeast	⅛ teaspoon salt
1 cup potato water	Flour

Take the hot water and make mush by adding enough corn meal. Then dissolve yeast in warm water. Mix remaining ingredients together to make a sponge. Then add salt and stir in enough flour to make a stiff dough. Set to rise in a warm place. When double in bulk, roll out in biscuit form and bake in a moderate oven until brown.

★ ★ ★

WOOD STAIN

You can color unfinished wood with a solution of green walnut hulls, boiled in a basin. After putting this on, take a mild lye solution and apply as a fixer.

FRITTERS

Here's some cookin that covers a heap of territory. I guess a-body thinks first of such vittles as corn fritters, apple fritters, green termaters, and so on. We aim to give you what's called the basic recipe and let you handle the makins.

★　　★　　★

FRITTER BATTER

1 cup flour
1½ teaspoons baking powder
2 tablespoons sugar

½ cup milk
¼ teaspoon salt
1 egg

When frying fritters of raw vegetables or fruit, have the fat hot enough to brown a cube of bread in one minute. Now of course if you're using canned corn, it takes around 45 seconds over hot heating.

Fat should be deep enough to cover the fritters. Each fritter will sink at first, then rise as baking powder acts. That's when you start turning the fritters to make all sides brown. Most fritters are done in five minutes. Take care and don't put too many fritters in at one time, so that the grease pops over.

For fruit, cut into small pieces and roll in sugar, powder if you have some around. Then dip in batter before sugar dissolves. Then fry.

For vegetables or meat fritters, dip into batter and then drip by spoonfulls into the pan or kettle. Best to use pan or deep skillet.

★　　★　　★

WEATHER SIGNS

If corn shucks are thick and tougher than ordinary, there's a hard winter ahead.

Green wood in fireplace will pop like somebody trompin snow afore a blizzard comes.

Whirlwinds mean dry weather.

11

HONEY MUFFINS

Honey sweetenin is always something special. Mountain folks like sourwood and poplar honey, while others like mixtures that bees know how to make. Be shore to strain honey from the comb when you use it in cookin.

RECIPE

1 cup butter
1 cup honey
2 cups flour
1 cup sugar

1 cup sour cream
1 teaspoon soda
½ teaspoon salt
1 egg

You stir all ingredients in then bake in muffin pans which are greased and coated with flour.

★   ★   ★

SALT RISIN BREAD

Afore there was store bought yeast cakes, Grandmaw had her own way of making bread rise. Some used hops of vines they growed, mashed taters, corn meal and salt to make cakes. Others used taters, salt and meal. Here's an old timer recipe:

3 medium potatoes
3 tablespoons corn meal
1 teaspoon sugar
Flour
4 cups boiling water
2 cups lukewarm milk

1 cup water
Pinch of baking soda
Pinch of salt
2 tablespoons melted
shortening

Peel and slice potatoes, add corn meal, sugar, salt and boiling water. Wrap in heavy cloth, cover and keep in a warm place overnight. Take out potatoes, add milk, soda, salt and shortening. Now you put in enough flour to make dough stiff when kneading. Form into loaves. Put into greased pans, cover and let dough rise twice in size. Bake in oven at 400 degrees. This makes four loaves.

★   ★   ★

Drop a horse hair into a rain barrel and it will start swimmin in a couple of days.

FRUIT COBBLER

You can use two tablespoons of honey instead of sugar for this.

RECIPE

2 cups flour
½ teaspoon salt
4 teaspoon baking powder
1 tablespoon sugar

½ cup fat
enough sweet milk to make dough

For berries, apples or peaches, put a layer of fruit on baking dish bottom, then a layer of pastry, according to recipe. Add another layer of fruit. Cover with pastry and bake at 425 F. for 25 minutes, or until crust is browned.

★　　★　　★

SWEET MILK WAFFLES

Griddle cakes and waffles hit the spot when they're yanked fresh off the stove. But you have to have waffle iron or griddle heated just right and well greased. Just keep that in mind.

RECIPE

2½ cups flour
4½ teaspoons baking powder
3 eggs

1½ cups milk
½ cup melted butter.

Pour batter from a pitcher into center of iron until half full and allow it to spread to the edge and start bubbling. Bake 2 to 3 minutes. Let stand a few minutes before serving.

★　　★　　★

BATTER CAKES

Some folks call them pancakes. They're good, whatever name you call them.

4 cups whole wheat flour
3 cups milk
1 teaspoon salt

4 teaspoons baking powder
2 eggs
4 tablespoons shortening

Combine ingredients in bowl and beat till light. Cook on hot griddle.

SOURDOUGH CAKES

I've heard them called yeast cakes 'cause they have to ferment ahead of cookin.

RECIPE

Starter makins
1 package yeast
1 teaspoon sugar

1 teaspoon salt
2 cups lukeware potato water
2 cups flour

Put water softened yeast with the rest in bowl and set for 48 hours. If you keep starter cold it will last for a wad of pancake makins.

Here's the actual cookin mix —

2 cups starter
2 cups lukewarm water

2½ cups flour
1 tablespoon sugar

You let this set overnight. To make cakes, add these

¼ cups evaporated milk
½ teaspoon salt

1 teaspoon soda
2 teaspoons sugar

Now mix, let stand five minutes then pour on hot griddle.

★   ★   ★

BUCKWHEAT CAKES

Besides good battercakes, buckwheat blooms make an awful tangy honey.

RECIPE

1 package yeast
2 cups lukewarm water
1½ cups flour

¾ cup sweet milk
¼ teaspoon salt
1 cup buckwheat flour

Soak yeast in water. Mix in flour and set overnight. Before cooking, add sweet milk, salt and buckwheat flour to make thin batter. Cook on hot griddle.

★   ★   ★

If a young un gits the earache, boil a swatch of sheep wool, drain the oil and put in the ear that hurts.

BLACKBERRY POPOVERS

There just ain't any way to keep blackberrys from makin good eatin if you treat them halfway right.

RECIPE

1 cup flour
½ teaspoon salt
1 tablespoon sugar

2 eggs
1 cup milk

Use egg beater or mixer until bubbles show. Fill hot greased baking cups 2/3 full. Bake 25 minutes at 440 F. Popovers should double in size and be dry and hollow. Custard cups do right well. Be sure to put cups on a pan to keep bottoms from browning.

Cut slit in side of popover and put in sugared berries.

★ ★ ★

POOR VALLEY WAFFLES

You'll find buttermilk waffles makes a tolerable good change for morning eatin.

2½ cups flour
1 teaspoon salt
1 teaspoon soda
3 eggs

2 cups buttermilk
½ cup melted butter or
margarine
1 teaspoon baking powder

Sift together dry ingredients. Add beaten yolks, buttermilk and melted butter. Fold in beaten egg white last. You can add ½ teaspoon vanilla if you like.

★ ★ ★

PRESERVED EGGS

In early times, wimmen folks preserved hen eggs a long time by puttin them in lime water, in crocks or even barrels. The usual amount was one pound of lime to a gallon of water.

TAME AND WILD MEAT COOKINS

EAST TENNESSEE FRIED CHICKEN

They used to say, "Neighbors are 'spectin company."
Then they just caught a chicken and wrung its head off.

RECIPE

1 cup flour
2 teaspoons salt
Dash of black pepper

Cut chicken into pieces,
wash well.

Put a half inch of cooking fat in pan and let it get hot.
Place chicken in. Keep turning till both sides are walnut
brown. Now cover pan and cook at slow heat 20 to 25
minutes.

Some folks put a tang in the cooking fat or oil by drop-
ping in a tablespoon of diced celery and a thin slice of onion.
Personally, I like plain chicken flavor.

"WE'LL HAVE CHICKEN AND DUMPLINS WHEN SHE COMES,"

This is a real company dinner fixin.

RECIPE

Two pounds of chicken meat cut up real good. Sprinkle
or roll in flour and sear in hot fat. Cover with water and
simmer until tender — from two to three hours. Now the
dumplins —

2 cups flour
4 teaspoons baking powder
1 teaspoon sugar

½ teaspoon salt
Milk or cold water enough to
make stiff drop batter.

This ought to make a quart, and you can use meat
stock with the water. Sift flour and baking powder until mix
drops from a spoon. Cook 12 minutes. Get the stew boiling
before you drop in the dumpling mix. Keep boiling until
dumplings are cooking. Don't get curious and lift the boiler
top till cooking time is over.

16

FINE MEAT COOKIN

What's the first thing you put on your plate? Meat, of course. Tame or wild. Maybe you like hog meat, and again, maybe you'd ruther have cow meat or chicken. I guess that's why wimmen folks learn early to make so many different dishes.

★　　★　　★

MOUNTAIN FRIED STEAK

Round steak's the best. Pound the daylights out of a slice for some folks, and it won't be hard on teeth.

1 pound steak	1 tablespoon fat
1 teaspoon salt	½ cup water
¼ cup flour	1 onion cut fine

Make your steak cuts, roll in flour and salt. After that, brown in skillet after you put in fat. Pour in water, cover pan or skillet and simmer till steaks are tender.

Onions in the leftover go well with flour and milk as gravy.

★　　★　　★

ROAST MEAT

Follow these rules for beef and pork rib and loin cuts.

Season with salt and pepper. Place fat side up on rack in open roasting pan. Needs no water and don't baste. Roast in slow oven 300 to 350 degrees till done. Don't let the meat get down in the drippings. Don't use dry method if meat cuts are not tender.

★　　★　　★

If a hoot owl comes to your winder three nights in a row, somebody close to you will die.

★　　★　　★

Possums was the meanest cusses around a henhouse. They'd crawl up a roost, git beside a hen, then crowd her till she fell off. When that happened, goodbye hen.

17

PIG'S FEET

Naturally, you have to clean pig's feet downright good. After all the scraping and such, put in a pot and cover with salt water. Now boil till the meat is so tender it slips off.

★　　★　　★

CHICKEN, HUNTERS' STYLE

Don't know what they was huntin, but what they et was somethin to talk about.

RECIPE

1 2½ pound broiling chicken	½ teaspoon pepper
½ cup salad oil	½ cup minced parsley
3 tablespoons vinegar	½ cup minced onion.
½ teaspoon salt	Fresh parsley

Split chicken as for broiling. Mix the oil, vinegar, salt, pepper, parsley and onion and put in a medium sized shallow dish. Lay chicken in this for at least an hour, turning it. Pour a little of the vingar and oil mixture over. Cover from time to time. Then put in well greased baking pan. closely and bake in a hot oven, 375 degrees for 30 minutes. Uncover to brown, allowing about 15 minutes longer. Garnish fresh parsley.

★　　★　　★

WILD DUCK

A mallard or canvasback can be roasted with or without stuffin. You can also git up an argument over usin apple stuffin or plain cornmeal based stuffin. Reckon it depends on your taste. Here's a base recipe:

2 mallard ducks	Salt and pepper
4 bacon strips	Spices.

Season ducks with salt and pepper, inside and out. Now for the two ways to cook them.

APPLE STUFFIN

Use three apples, sliced thin with peeling on. Use two apples sliced thin to line for stuffing and also in baking pan around ducks.

For the stuffing, use the other sliced apple, three cups cornbread, stale; 1 onion chopped fine; 3 tablespoons melted butter or margarine, 1 teaspoon salt.

If you like, sprinkle some unseeded raisins when you mix ingredients and add enough water to moisten thoroughly. Stuff duck and put the rest outside in pan. Put two strips of bacon over each duck. Pour a cup and half into pan and cook at 350 degrees until meat is tender. Keep a watch on the water.

★   ★   ★

CORN MEAL STUFFIN

Since chestnuts got hit by the blight, chestnut stuffin is mighty scarce, for you have to buy furriners' nuts. But sage and cornmeal has been the standby a long time. It goes with game, like wild duck. And if quail is roasted, drippings do fine in stuffin. Same goes for guinea hens, which ain't so tame as some folks would think.

RECIPE

Best broth is chicken to start with. Put 3 cups of it and heat in pan. Takes almost a full cup of corn meal which you pour into the pan while stirring. Cook this ten minutes then put in around two and a half cups of bread crumbs, a beaten egg, 2/3 cup chopped celery and two or three little onions chopped real fine. Before you start mixing, put in as much sage as you like, along with the salt and pepper.

★   ★   ★

When I was a boy I slept upstairs under a shingle roof. Many a mornin in winter snow sifted on the top bed cover. Them was the times I dressed under the quilts and scooted fur a fire.

ROAST GUINEA

A pot-er-ack hen full grown has a wild game taste. We ain't advisin how to catch one, 'cept when you know where they roost, it's better to pick one out after dark.

RECIPE

Prepare as you would a hen. Dust with salt and pepper. Use cornmeal stuffing but add 1 tablespoon cooking oil.

Some people use almost a tablespoon of ham fat poured over the fowl after stuffing. You have to watch to keep meat from getting too dry. Cook in oven at 500 for twelve minutes, than down to 400 for the rest of the hour.

★　　★　　★

BUTTERED TURNIPS

Here's somethin that goes fine with game dishes.

RECIPE

3 bunches young turnips　　1/3 cup melted butter
salt　　　　　　　　　　　1 tablespoon minced parsley
½ teaspoon sugar

Peel turnips, dust with salt and cook tender. Caramelize sugar. Melt butter in same pan. Add parsley and pour this over turnips. Let stand ten minutes before serving.

★　　★　　★

WILD GAME AND FISH

I reckon the taste for wild game was passed on naturally. Mountain men once had to provide by gun and fishhook, 'cept what he trapped. The wimmen folks learnt how to make some fine dishes too.

★　　★　　★

QUAIL

When I was a boy, I'd take my pointer and hit bird country real early. My Grandmaw liked roast quail. We-uns at home fried them.

ROAST QUAIL

Season the dressed birds with salt and pepper. Melted butter goes best in the baking pan and some poured on the quail. You can use thin slices of bacon over the birds. Put in hot oven and bake 15 minutes at 450. Cut to 350 til quail are chestnut brown. If you want extra tenderness, baste several times with water and melted butter. Some folks use the gravy mixed with flour to thicken.

★ ★ ★

FRIED QUAIL

Fry like a young chicken, except use deeper fat.

★ ★ ★

VENISON ROAST

After you cut up the carcass, about the first job is to wash with vingar water several times. Use plenty of salt, mixed with chopped onions, and some spices. Now put the roast in a pot on top of the stove and brown afore puttin in pan. Put in close to two cups water. A few strips of bacon, cut thick, should go on top. Now drop in a good pinch of black pepper. Some folks like the tang of chopped celery added. Cut the celery fine. It takes three full hours in roasting pan with oven at 325 degrees.

★ ★ ★

SQUIRREL AND SWEET TATERS

Aunt Elviry would take a mess of squirrels, cut them up and parboil in mild salt water. Then she would drain off water, flour and pepper, and put in a roastin pan at slow heat. About the time the meat was gettin hot, she plunked in sweet taters already part boiled. Lots of folks might not like to brush taters with brown sugar, but she did.

★ ★ ★

Does anything ease your thirst more 'n cold spring water drunk from a long handle gourd which has been used a long time?

FRIED RABBIT

Cottontails have tender meat when full grown and they're fed well. And they don't take long to cook up.

RECIPE

1 cup flour
1 teaspoon salt
Pepper to taste

Cooking fat
1 diced onion
Juice of ¼ lemon

Roll cut up pieces in flour, salt and pepper. Brown the meat in four to five tablespoons cooking fat. After that, put in diced onions and lemon juice. Cook till done.

Some folks like stewed rabbit, which needs some care in fixin. Best to soak cut up pieces in a mix of twice the vinegar as water and let stand overnight. You put in some flour, and salt and pepper to taste. Stew in pan till done.

★   ★   ★

TARRAPIN DISH

Now I've heard about tarrapin dishes in hot countries near the ocean. Them's great big sea turtles, not tarrapins. All my life I heard folks insist they liked stewed tarrapin. Well sir, when I saw them plunk the pore things alive into boilin water, I began to lose my yearnin. Why, it took hours to git the things ready, and they tasted sort of like stewed chicken or guinea. So, if you want to fool somebody, cut up hunks of pork backstrip fresh and a fat hen. Now pick out some spices, black pepper, a little vinegar and pour in some wine, sour kind the best. Now to top it off, pour in whole milk—a cupfull, some butter, and even some boiled eggs. I'll bet whoever eats that goes aroun braggin it's the tastiest tarrapin he ever et.

★   ★   ★

In most of the old folks' gardens, a few hills of pomegrannies were planted. The yeller striped little melons was good only fur sweet smells. They'd scent up the whole house when put around in saucers.

22

FROG LEGS

City man moved near the mill pond once and heard maybe two or three bullfrogs goin. So he writ his cousin in the city he wanted to sell frog legs by the barrel. You know what? He caught six the first month.

RECIPE

Remove skin, wash and cut off feet. Soak an hour in salt water. Beat an egg lightly. Salt and pepper legs. Dip in meal or crumbs, then in eggs. Dip again in meal. Fry in deep fat. Be sure to drain off all grease when finished.

★   ★   ★

FRIED FISH

There's a thousand little differences in frying small fish — the kind usually caught. Still, there are some things to do, no matter what you add accordin to your taste. Some catches, like catfish, take more meal and more cooking fat than, say bream.

Clean fish and scale. Wash in cold water. If the fish is big, cut into sections. With smaller ones, simply split. Salt, then roll in meal and flour, half and half. Use from a half to an inch, according to size. Turn to brown both sides.

★   ★   ★

BAKED FISH WITH TANGY SAUCE

1½ pounds fish filet any kind	juice from ½ lemon
	Pinch of black pepper
1½ teaspoon salt	
1 quart ripe tomatoes	2 tablespoons lemon juice
1 teaspoon sugar	Pinch of nutmeg
1 teaspoon salt	2 cloves
1 tablespoon chopped onions	1 sprig celery leaves
1 teaspoon Worchestershire Sauce	1 tablespoon butter
	1 tablespoon flour

Put fish on greased glass or earthenware platter. Sprinkle with lemon juice and dust with salt and pepper. Pour the sauce over. Cover and bake 30 minutes at 350, or the fish is brown. If you like, garnish with greens.

BARBECUED CHICKEN

We-uns like barbecued kid, pig and chicken. Of the three, chicken gits more pop'lar. Now you can barbecue chicken on an outdoor grill or in an oven. First, here's a barbecue sauce recipe for two broiler chickens. Naturally, if you barbecue, say a half dozen broilers, you'd multiply the amount of sauce ingredients by three.

★   ★   ★

SAUCE RECIPE

¼ cup mustard
¼ cup prepared mustard
¼ cup unsulphured molases
   (Them's New Orleans)
¼ cup corn oil

¼ cup vinegar
2 tablespoons Worcestershire
   sauce
1 teaspoon tabasco.

To cook in oven, sprinkle cavity of each chicken with salt. Then truss fowl. Blend mustard and molasses. Stir in oil, vinegar, Worcestershire sauce and tabasco. Take a baking pan and line with aluminum foil. Brush chickens with barbecue mix. Now keep temperature at 350 degrees and cook for an hour and 15 minutes, or until tender. Brush chickens several times with barbecue mixture.

★   ★   ★

The way our chicken barbecuin friend Bill Sewell does it, is on top of the ground. Bill finds concrete blocks stacked on top of the ground is a sight easier than diggin a pit. He puts bars acrost the top and builds his charcoal fire underneath, so that a steady heat does the job, not to close. If you ain't got enough bars, use wire mesh to put the chicken halves on. Bastin them with the sauce is like with a spit or oven. But there's something about open fire barbecuing that please the folks. You got to have patience and turn the chickens often.

PUDDINS AND PIES

When folks around here talk of Indians, they usually mean Cherokees, 'cause they were the ones who drove off all other tribes. Cherokees gave us a lot of names fur dishes the wimmen folks adopted. Here's one.

CHEROKEE PUDDIN

6 tablespoons corn meal
1 quart milk
½ pint cold water
½ cup suet chopped
3 tablespoons brown sugar
1 cup molasses

1 teaspoon soda
1 tablespoon ginger
½ teaspoon cinnamon
½ teaspoon nutmeg
4 eggs

Boil the milk, put cold water in the meal to wet it. Pour meal into the boiling milk along with salt and suet. Boil for a quarter hour and keep stirring. If skim forms, remove it. You add ½ cup cold milk, sugar and molasses. Stir the soda first in the molasses. Then add the spices, beat the yolks and the last thing is to put in the stiff beaten whites. Grease or butter the pan and bake for an hour. Because there'll be a little whey, let it cool for a while.

★   ★   ★

BLACKBERRY OR DEWBERRY PUDDIN

You be shore the berries are real fresh.

RECIPE

2 cups flour
1/3 cup butter
2 cups sugar
2 cups real hot water

1 teaspoon salt
2 teaspoons baking powder
1 cup milk
2 cups berries

Work sugar and butter (or margarine) together. Put in flour with baking powder, salt and milk. Stir good. Pour berries on top, then 1 cup sugar and 2 cups water. Bake an hour.

25

APPLE PUDDIN

More puddins are et than cake, 'cause, mostly, puddins can be made with leftovers.

RECIPE

1 egg
¾ cup sugar
2 tablespoons flour
1¼ teaspoon baking powder
Pinch of salt

cup of chopped walnuts
or hickory nuts
½ cup chopped apples
1 teaspoon vanilla

Beat sugar and eggs smooth, then put in flour, baking powder, salt. Stir into egg mixture. Bake in a greased pan at 325 F. for 30 minutes. If you like topping, use whipped or ice cream.

★   ★   ★

PORE MAN'S PUDDIN

2 cupfulls cold boiled rice
3 cupfulls hot milk
¼ cup molasses
½ teaspoon nutmeg

¼ cup raisins
1 tablespoon margarine
1 teaspoonfull salt

Mix rice and hot milk. Add molasses, raisins, margarine, salt and nutmeg. Bake at 350 F. in greased pan for an hour. Stir after the first half hour.

★   ★   ★

UP THE HOLLER PUDDIN

If you don't grow barley, maybe some neighbor has a little on hand. This don't take much.

RECIPE

4 cupfulls milk
½ cup barley
1/3 cupfull honey

½ teaspoon salt
½ teaspoon cinnamon
1 tablespoon shortening

Wash barley. Mix ingredients and pour into buttered pudding dish. Bake 3 hours in a 300 degree oven, stirring 3 times the first hour so as to keep barley from settling. Let stand an hour to partially soften.

SOUR MILK PUDDIN

This is a real old timer. And it's still good.

RECIPE

1 cupfull stale cornbread
2 cupfulls sour milk
1 egg
4 tablespoon molasses

½ teaspoon soda
½ cupfull raisins
¼ teaspoon cinnamon

Crumble bread and soak in milk 30 minutes. Add beaten egg, raisins, soda and spice and bake at 325 until mix begins to set. Then spread the molasses over the top and bake until a firm crust forms.

★   ★   ★

SWEET TATER PUDDIN

3 large sweet potatoes
1 cupfull sugar
1 cupfull milk

1 egg
1 tablespoon melted butter
1 teaspoon grated nutmeg.

Grate potatoes, add sugar and milk and mix. Beat in egg and add butter and nutmeg. Use a well greased, shallow pan. Bake at 350 till brown. If you put preserves or such on top, brown at 300 degrees.

★   ★   ★

MAPLE LAYER CAKE

You'll like the flavor of this.

RECIPE

3 eggs
1 cupfull soft maple sugar
1 cupfull flour
½ teaspoon salt

1 teaspoon baking soda
1 cupfull cream
¼ cupfull grated maple sugar

Beat egg yolks till light. Add the soft maple sugar and flour sifted with the salt and baking powder. Fold in last, whites of the eggs beaten very stiff. Mix at once and bake for 30 minutes in two greased and floured layer cake pans at 320 degrees. Put together with the creamed whipped and sweetened with the grated maple sugar. Sprinkle top layer with powdered sugar.

PIES AND SUCH

Nobody knows who first invented pies, but I'll bet it was close to Garden of Eden time, when the first sweetenin was learnt.

★   ★   ★

SORGHUM MOLASSES PIE

1 cup sugar
2 cups molasses
3 hen eggs

1 tablespoon melted butter
juice of 1 lemon
Smidgeon of nutmeg

Just mix everything and heat up. Then bake in moderate oven.

★   ★   ★

HALF MOON PIES

When I was a young un, nothing went better'n a half moon pie of dried peaches or apples, cold or hot.

RECIPE

Make a nice pie dough about the span of thumb and fingers (6 inches). Have your dried fruit soaked, then laid out. Sprinkle white or brown sugar when you spread fruit on half the dough, then fold over. Use a fork to go around the folded edge of the dough, mashing kind of easy. Fry in deep fat. Around 370 to 380 degrees till puffin and brownin satisfies you. If you got too much grease, let pies set on paper towels a spell.

★   ★   ★

APPLE OR RHUBARB PIE

Cut either into small bits. With rhubarb git rid of stringy skins. Use a cup of sugar, ½ teaspoon cinnamon, ¼ teaspoon nutmeg, a little lemon juice and a dab of butter. Some folks like a third cup of molasses with the sugar. Rhubarb or apples, 4 cups. Bake moderate.

GREEN TERMATER PIE

Come to think of it, you can do a heap with termaters. They fry good when green or ripe. They go into a mess of recipes when ripe. But you never figgered green termaters could make such a good pie. Just try it.

RECIPE

2 cups chopped green
  tomatoes
½ cup brown sugar
2 tablespoons cider vinegar
½ teaspoon cinnamon
½ cup chopped raisins

3 tablespoons melted butter
  or margarine
½ teaspoon salt
3 cloves
¼ teaspoon mace

Cover tomatoes and boil quickly. Drain then add other ingredients. Put in pie plate lined with rich pie crust. Put on top crust and slash to let steam escape. Crimp crust edges. Bake from 35 to 40 minutes in hot oven, 375 degrees.

★ ★ ★

PIE PASTRY

When pie crusts and bottoms ain't just right, it hurts the whole business. Right here we-uns figgered a word about good eatin pie pastry is worth puttin in.

★ ★ ★

REGULAR PASTRY

1¼ cups sifted flour
¼ teaspoon salt

5 to 6 tablespoons fat
3 tablespoons cold water

Sift flour, measure and sift flour and salt. Cut in fat with two knives or a potato masher. Sprinkle water over the top and cut it in quickly. Then press the dough into a ball without kneading it. Roll out on lightly floured board. Roll onto the rolling pin, then unroll on pie plate. Prick with fork to stop bubbles. Edge with a fork, or crimp with fingers. Bake at 450 for 10-12 minutes. If the pastry browns too fast, reduce to 425 degrees.

SQUASH PIE

Just use cooked and mashed squshed in place of pumpkin. Other ingredients same.

★   ★   ★

FRESH APPLE PIE

Best thing about this recipe is that it's got that juicy top crust.

RECIPE

3 cups coarsely chopped
  apples
1½ cups sugar
2 Tablespoons flour

¼ teaspoon salt
1 tablespoon lemon juice
4 tablespoons melted butter

Mix all ingredients in order given. Place unbaked pie shell which has been sprinkled with one heaping tablespoon of sugar and one tablespoon of butter. Cover with pie dough strips, crisscross. Brush with melted butter. Bake in 350 degree oven for 40 minutes.

★   ★   ★

DEEP DISH APPLE PIE

This un comes powerful near o being a cobbler, for individuals.

1 quart chopped apples
1 cup granulated sugar
½ teaspoon cinnamon.

1 tablespoon melted butter
  or margarine
Milk and rich pie crust

RECIPE

Grease individual baking dishes. Fill three-fourths with the apple, sugar, melted butter and cinnamon mixed. Top with pie crust, pressing it about the edges with a fork. Slash the crust center. Brush with milk and bake at 350 to 375 Takes about 35 minutes.

★   ★   ★

If the feathers in your piller form circles, somebody's going to die with his head on it.

FRUIT WHIP PIE

You can use fresh fruit, canned fruit, dried fruit in this recipe.

2 cups fruit pulp   ¾ cup sugar
3 egg whites   ½ cup nuts

Put fruit pulp through coarse strainer. Add sugar, nuts and egg whites beaten stiff. Pour into pie shell. Bake 20 minutes in slow oven (300). Cool and cover with whipped cream.

★   ★   ★

CLINCH MOUNTAIN VINEGAR PIE

So many folks like our vinegar pies we just had to give you our favorite.

RECIPE

1 cup sugar   1 cup water
2 eggs   Small lump butter or
2 tablespoons vinegar   margarine
2 tablespoons flour (or   ½ teaspoon lemon extract
   corn starch

Combine sugar, eggs, vinegar, flour (or corn starch), and water in double boiler and cook until thick and smooth, stirring occasionally. Just before removing from heat stir in small lump of butter and some lemon extract. Pour into baked pie shell. If desired, the pie may be topped with frosting or whipped cream.

★   ★   ★

When Grandmaw used a wood stove, us kids didn't dare go through the kitchen when a cake was bakin. And I've heard grownups catch it when they shook a cake down.

★   ★   ★

There ain't a time in mountain country when there's nothing to look at. In the spring it's wild flowers and purty tree blooms like silver bells and sarvices, just to mention a few. In the summer, it's grand. And in cold weather, man, you-uns come.

CAKES, TEACAKES AND SUCH

OLD FASHION STACK CAKE

Whenever talk gits aroun to good things Grandmaw used to bake, somebody ups and mentions stack cake. I know persons who stoop to usin apple sauce instead of the real thing—dried apples. This recipe is the real thing.

RECIPE

1 pound dried tart apples
1 cup brown sugar
½ cup sugar

2 teaspoons cinnamon
½ teaspoon cloves
½ teaspoon allspice

Wash and cook apples until tender. Mash thoroughly. Add sugar and spices.

★   ★   ★

CAKE

4 cups unsifted flour
1 cup sugar
4 teaspoons baking powder
½ teaspoon baking soda
1 teaspoon salt

2 eggs
½ cup soft butter
1 cup buttermilk
2 teaspoons vanilla

Sift 3 and ¾ cups flour into a bowl. Add remaining ingredients in order given. Mix quickly into soft dough. Divide into 6 parts. Use remaining ¼ cup flour to roll out dough. Bake in 9 inch cake pans at 450 degrees until slightly brown.

As you take cake from oven, spread each layer with the apple mixture. Don't put apples on top layer. Put in covered container at least 12 hours before cutting.

★   ★   ★

My folks, Aunt 'Phelia used to keep gingercakes in a white crock with a blue top. I still recollect how the tang of those cakes would come out when I'd take off the crock lid.

DRIED APPLE PUDDIN

It's pow'ful easy to make.

RECIPE

½ cup cornmeal
1 cup flour
1 teaspoon salt
2 teaspoons baking powder
1 teaspoon soda

1½ cups buttermilk
2 cups dried apples mashed
and sweetened with corn
syrup or honey

Mix in soft dry ingredients. Add buttermilk to make batter thick enough to drop from spoon on a hot, greased griddle. Make 12 cakes. When serving, put mashed apples between 2 cakes and sprinkle powder sugar light on top. Serve hot with thin cream.

★　　★　　★

GINGER CAKES

1 cup sorghum molasses
1 teaspoon soda
¼ cup warm water
¾ sugar

1 teaspoon salt
Pinch of pepper
2½ teaspoons ground ginger
4 cups cake flour

Dissolve soda in water, then add ingredients in the order given. Add a little more flour if needed. Roll all or part on a floured board. Bake ten minutes 350 to 375 degrees. Should make close to eight dozen cakes unless you want them big.

★　　★　　★

REBEL CAKE

This uns for folks who git tired of eggs, milk and butter and still want cake.

RECIPE

2 cupfulls brown sugar
2 cupfulls hot water
2 tablespoons shortening
1 teaspoon salt
1 package seedless raisins

1 teaspoon cinnamon
1 teaspoon cloves
3 cupfulls flour
1 teaspoon soda

Boil together with sugar, water, lard, salt, raisins and spices for five minutes. When cold, add flour and soda dissolved in a teaspoon of hot water. This makes two loaves. Bake about 45 minutes in a 325 F oven.

BLACKBERRY CAKE

Best to use fresh picked berries.

RECIPE

½ cupfull shortening
1 cupfull sugar
2 eggs
½ teaspoon cloves
2 cupfulls flour

1 teaspoon cinnamon
½ teaspoon salt
1 teaspoon soda
1 cup fresh cooked berries

Cream shortening and sugar. Add beaten eggs, holding one egg white for icing. Sift dry ingredients and add mixture. Add berries last. Cook 1¼ hours in greased and floured pan. Hold temperature at 325 degrees. Frost with boiled icing.

★   ★   ★

WEDDIN CAKE

If you want somethin special when somebody's marryin up, try this un.

RECIPE

2 cups butter
3 cupfulls brown sugar
10 eggs
4 cupfulls pastry flour
1 teaspoon soda
1 teaspoon cinnamon
1 teaspoon nutmeg
1 teaspoon mace

½ teaspoon allspice
½ teaspoon cloves
¼ teaspoon salt
½ cupfull sweet cider
    or grape juice
1 cupfull molasses
2 pounds white currants
1 pound citron

Cream together butter and brown sugar. Add well beaten eggs. Mix and sift together three and a half cupfulls flour, soda, salt and spices. Add these dry ingredients to the first mixture, first with the cider, then the molasses. Weigh out currants, slice citron real thin and mix with the rest of the flour. Add to the cake. Beat well and pour into three well greased and floured bake pans. Bake at 275 degrees for three hours.

AUNT LIZZIE'S BLACK CHOCOLATE CAKE

To this day I don't know if it was the cake or the crunchy, thick icin that made it so good.

3½ squares bitter chocolate
1 cup milk
1 egg and an egg yolk extra
2 tablespoons butter

1 cup sugar
1 teaspoon vanilla
1⅛ cups cake flour
¾ teaspoon soda

Melt chocolate over hot water. Stir in a half cup of the milk, combine with the beaten yolk, stirring until it thickens. Add flour and salt beaten together and the ramaining milk, then add butter and sugar and put in mixing bowl. Add vanilla, beat in the soda dissolved in a teaspoon of milk, and fold in the egg white, whipped stiff. Put in oiled cake pans. Cook in moderate oven at 350 degrees for 30 minutes. When cold, cover with thick icing.

★   ★   ★

THICK CHOCOLATE ICING

¼ pound sweet chocolate
2 tablespoons cream

Sifted confectioner's
sugar (as needed)

Melt chocolate in double boiler. Add cream. Beat in confectioner's sugar until icing is creamy and thick enough to spread.

★   ★   ★

DRIED APPLE CAKE

2 cups dried apples
1 cup sugar
2 eggs
3 cups or more of flour
2/3 cup baking powder

1 cup raisins
1 cup molasses
1 cup milk
1 teaspoon soda — level
Nutmeg and cinnamon

Soak apples in water long enough to make soft. Then chop them to about the size of raisins, and boil them for fifteen minutes in the molasses. Dissolve the soda in a little hot water, and put this in the molasses when cold. Then mix in all other ingredients, beat well, and pour into cake pan. Bake in moderate oven till done.

BUTTERMILK CAKE

If you like something with a different flavor here's a good recipe:

RECIPE

½ cup margarine	1 teaspoon nutmeg
1 cup sugar	1½ teaspoons soda
½ cup molasses	2 cups pastry flour
2 eggs	1 cup buttermilk
1 teaspoon cinnamon	¾ cup raisins
¼ teaspoon salt	¾ cup nut meats

Cream together margarine and sugar. Add molasses and eggs well beaten. Sift together dry ingredients, keeping back enough flour to dust the raisins. Add this alternately with the buttermilk to the mixture. Chop nuts and raisins fine, dust with flour and add to mixture. Beat well, pour into large loaf pan and bake at 350 degrees for about 45 minutes.

★　　★　　★

SOFT HONEY CAKE

First, find a bee tree. That is, if you or a neighbor ain't got beehives.

RECIPE

1 cup butter	4 cups flour
2 cups honey	2 teaspoons soda
2 eggs	1 teaspoon ginger
1 cup sour milk or buttermilk	1 teaspoon cinnamon
¼ teaspoon salt	

Cream butter and honey well. Add beaten eggs, sour milk, flour sifted with soda, spices and salt. Mix well and bake in two layers in a slow oven, 275 degrees, for about 30 minutes. Watch close, for honey cake burns very easily.

★　　★　　★

A feller who was too lazy not to boil honey comb for beeswax, didn't amount to much. Beeswax made thread last longer, shined furniture and leather sometimes. It was powerful handy.

HUCKLEBERRY CAKE

Wimmen liked to bake this when huckleberries was in season.

RECIPE

½ cup butter
1 cup sugar
3 eggs (beaten)
¾ cup milk

2 cups flour
2 teaspoons baking powder
1 cup huckleberries

Cream butter with sugar. Add eggs and milk. Sift together flour and baking powder, and add to mixture. Stir in a cup of huckleberries dredged with flour. Bake in a moderate oven (350 degrees) in a deep cake pan. Serve plain or with vanilla sauce.

★ ★ ★

CHOCOLATE UPSIDE DOWN CAKE

This is an old standby and we-uns have heard more 'n a dozen say it was theirs first.

RECIPE

PART 1:

1 cup flour
¾ cup sugar
2 tablespoons cocoa

2 teaspoons baking powder
¼ teaspoon salt

Sift together the above ingredients, then add ½ cup sweet milk and beat well. Then add 4 tablespoons shortening & 1 teaspoon vanilla and beat until fluffy. Mix in ½ cup nutmeats and pour into well greased and floured pan (about 7 x 10).

PART 2:

Combine ½ cup white sugar, ½ cup brown sugar, and 2 tablespoons cocoa in separate bowl. Mix well and sprinkle over top of cake batter. Pour 1 cup of cold water on top, and then bake in a moderate oven (357 degrees) for about 30 minutes. Leave this cake in pan until ready to serve. Cut into squares, then with pancake turner lift and turn each piece upside down. The icing will be on top.

37

BLACK WALNUT CAKE

One job we young uns hated to do was to hull walnuts. They was green and dyed skin and clothin. But when the walnuts dried out they sure had a place in the kitchen.

RECIPE

¾ cup shortening	¼ teaspoon salt
2 cups sugar	pinch of nutmeg
4 eggs	3 teaspoons baking powder
1½ cups black walnut meats	1 cup milk
¼ cup raisins	grated rind 1 orange
3 cups cake flour	¼ teaspoon lemon extract
Icing	¼ teaspoon orange extract

Cream the shortening. Beat in slowly sugar and add the eggs, unbeaten, one at a time. Put nutmeg and raisins through food chopper and add the flour, sifted with the salt, nutmeg and baking powder. Add to the mixture with the milk. Stir in orange rind and flavorings. Pour into oiled, square pan about 8 inches wide. Bake slowly at 350 degrees for 50 minutes. Cover with the walnut cream icing.

★   ★   ★

WALNUT CREAM ICING

¼ cup butter or margarine	2 tablespoons heated cream
2 cups confectioner's sugar	½ cup chopped walnuts
1 teaspoon vanilla	coarse
Pinch of salt	

Stir butter until creamy and gradually work in confectioner's sugar, vanilla and salt. Then add hot cream and beat in the second cup of confectioner's sugar. Stir in nuts and beat until creamy.

★   ★   ★

Ever go to an all day singin, and dinner on the grounds? When the wimmen folks began to lay out table cloths, either on plank tables or on the grass where it was shady, the menfolks would cut small limbs so as to brush off the flies. But is was shore fun.

38

BAKED APPLE BETTY

Betty's product used to be mighty popular with us young uns.

RECIPE

10 thin slices stale bread minus crusts
¼ cup butter
3 cups sliced apples
¾ cup seded raisins

¾ cup brown sugar
1 cup boiling water
Whipped or top cream or hard sauce

Grease baking dish and spread as lining. Combine apples, raisins and sugar and put a layer over the bread. Then cover with more bread which has been covered with butter, and add another layer of apple-raisins. Repeat process until ingredients are used. Top with dots of butter and pour the boiling water. Cover. Place in a hot oven, 375 degrees, for 30 minutes. Serve warm with sauce.

★ ★ ★

AUNT LIZZIE'S POUND CAKE

Bite for bite, most men like pound cake about as much as any kind wimmen can bake.

RECIPE

1 cupfull butter
2 cupfulls sugar
4 eggs
2 cupfulls pastry flour
¼ teaspoon salt

1 teaspoon cream of tartar
½ teaspoon soda
½ cupfull milk
1 teaspoon vanilla
¼ teaspoon mace

Cream together butter and sugar till very light, then add the egg yolks beaten until thick and lemon-colored. Beat again. Mix and sift together the flour, salt, cream of tartar and soda. Add to the first mixture along with the milk. Beat well, add the vanilla and mace, then fold in egg whites which have been stiffly beaten. Bake in greased and floured pan at 350 degrees for 45 minutes.

MAW'S GINGERBREAD

Like her gingercakes, Maw knew how to have somethin us young uns craved most any time.

1 cupfull brown sugar	2½ cupfuls pastry flour
½ cupful butter	½ teaspoonful soda
½ cupful cream	1 tablespoon ginger
2 eggs	½ teaspoon salt
1 cupful molasses	½ cupful milk

Cream butter (or margarine) and sugar together, add the cream and the eggs—the eggs well beaten. Then add molasses, sift the dry ingredients and add to the other mixture, along with the milk. Pour into a small dripping pan which has been well greased and floured. Bake in a 350 degree oven.

★　　★　　★

SALLY LUNN

Now I ain't shore where Sally Lunn lived, but this recipe shore does her memory honor.

RECIPE

2 cups milk	4 tablespoons sugar
1 cup fat	2 teaspoons salt
1 to 2 yeast cakes	6 cups fine flour
3 beaten eggs	

Scald milk and add fat and when fat melts, cool to hand temperature. Crumble in yeast, add beaten eggs, sugar and salt. Mix well and stir in flour. Beat thoroughly. Cover and let rise in a warm place until double in size. Punch down, spoon into greased 9 inch ring mold or pan and let double in size again.

Bake in moderate oven, 350 degrees for one hour. this recipe serves about 16 persons. Serve real hot with butter. Handle like angel food cake.

★　　★　　★

When the first katydid hollers, it's just six weeks till frost.

PRESERVES, PICKLIN AND SOUSE

WATERMELON PRESERVES

You need a watermelon with a thick rind, dead ripe so that it's mealy. That's how to start, after you've enjoyed the juicy, red heart. And folks, watermelon preserves made right just can't be beat.

RECIPE

Cut off the red part and skin the rind. Cut into pieces four to five inches. Put into boiling water five minutes. After that, plunk the pieces into lime water. That's to make them crisp. Soak for four hours. You make this lime water with one tablespoonful of slacked lime to one quart of water. After that drain then put in cold water. Now they're ready to put in the kettle. Cook just at the boiling point a half hour. Add three-fourths cup of sugar for each pound of rinds. Cook at slow heat — not boiling too much for twenty minutes. Now put in another three-forths cup of sugar and let things simmer around twenty minutes. Some folks add sugar syrup on top of this before putting in jars.

★ ★ ★

YELLOW TOMATO PRESERVES

You need the small kind. Some folks call them fig tomatoes. My grandmaw growed a special clump, and I still hanker for the taste of her preserves.

You blanch the tomatoes one minute, which means putting them into hot water till the skins are loose. Cool, then dip and peel. Here's the fixings:

1 quart water	2 quarts tomatoes
4 cups sugar	⅜ teaspoon ginger
¾ teaspoon cinnamon	½ lemon

Cook with water and half the sugar five minutes. Simmer maybe two hours. Add remaining sugar and spices and cook at 225 F. 20 to 30 minutes. Cool.

SWEET SPICED PEACHES

You can almost slurp these in one swallow, they're so good.

RECIPE

3 pounds peaches
2 pounds sugar (4 cups)
1 pint vinegar
1 cup water

2 ounces stick cinnamon
1 ounce whole cloves
½ ounce whole ginger

Blanch firm peaches in boiling water one minute. Chill, then drain and peel. Freestones can be halved and pitted. Boil 3 minutes if peaches are whole, and 1 minute if they're halved. Cool in syrup. Add rest of sugar and cook till tender and not mushy. Let stand for day, then drain off syrup and reheat. Pack in warm jars.

You can put up pears or apples same way. Don't peel crabapples, if you're putting them up. Eat them skin and all.

★   ★   ★

Drummer down at the county seat had a clock that's meant to run forever without winding. Uncle Ples said "somebody's always trying to take the fun out of life."

★   ★   ★

CORN RELISH

Mighty good when the winter wind is howlin.

RECIPE

1 dozen ears corn (2 qts-3 lbs)
1 head cabbage
3 red peppers
3 sweet green peppers
1 quart vinegar

1 cup water
1 cup sugar
2 teaspoons mustard
2 tablespoons salt
1 tablespoon celery seed

Blanch corn 2 minutes. Drop into cold water before cutting off cob. Chop peppers and cabbage. Cook all together 20 minutes. After you pack in jars simmer 25 minutes.

SOUSE MEAT

This is something that comes with cold weather and hog killin time. This recipe calls for a steam pressure cooker, which shore does cut down cookin time.

RECIPE

Scald, scrape and clean pig's feet. Sprinkle lightly with salt and leave for 4 hours. Wash feet again and put in pressure cooker with just enough water to cover them. Cook for 30 minutes at 15 pounds pressure. Let steam escape slowly before opening cooker. Pick out all bones. Strain liquid in which feet were cooked and remove the fat or the product will be too greasy. Combine meat and liquor. Season to taste with salt, pepper, allspice, cloves and a small amount of vinegar. Reheat to boiling, pack, seal and process. (90 minutes for packing in quart jars. Pressure canner at 10 pounds. (240 degrees)

★　　★　　★

GINGER PEARS

4 pounds sliced pears   2 ounces green ginger root
3 pounds sugar   2 lemons

Select hard, green pears. Peel and slice thin. Scrape ginger root into tiny pieces and squeeze a little lemon juice over it. Cover pears with the sugar and stand for a few hours. Then place them over a slow fire and simmer. Add the ginger root and the juice and grated rind of the lemons. When clear and very thick, remove from the fire and pour into sterilized jars or crocks.

★　　★　　★

PEACH AND ORANGE MARMALADE

On a hot biscuit! Man, oh Man!

RECIPE

Peel and stone peaches, two dozen in all. Wash and peel 4 oranges. Cut skins in thin strips and orange inside into bits. Combine and add 3½ pounds sugar. Stand overnight. To process, bring mixture gradually to boiling point then simmer gently until thick. About 2 hours.

43

CLINCH MOUNTAIN OLIVES

*No, they ain't real olives. You have to use green toma-
toes no bigger 'n a marble. Well, maybe a little larger.
These make fine relishes with any sort of meal.*

RECIPE

½ pound salt to ½ gal. water   Grape leaves
½ gallon tomatoes, small   Dill heads
   and green   1 tablespoon celery seed
2 large onions   1 tablespoon ground mustard
2 tablespoons vinegar

Brine tomatoes 5 to 6 days. Add onions second day.
Drain in water twice. Take mustard, celery and vingar. Mix
in 2 cupfulls water. Put tomatoes, onions and other mixture
into open vessel and run up to boiling point, then remove
and cool at once.

Use old fashioned crock. Place grape leaves in bottom,
then put in mixture, adding brine to stand even with tomatoes. Now spread dill on top. Last thing, spread rest of
grape leaves on top. Seal lid after three days with paraffin
wax.

★   ★   ★

AUNT LIZA'S PICKLED OKRA

*Reckon few people have a fine spring handy like Aunt
Liza, so where she plunked her okra into the spring, you
just use a tub or large bucket.*

RECIPE

Take uncapped okra and put in brine thick enough to
float an egg. Let stay till fall. Soak okra in water a day and
night. Now put okra into kettle and pour scalding hot apple
vinegar over okra. After about an hour, put okra in jars or
crocks. Handled this way, okra will be green and crisp.

★   ★   ★

*A poultice of dried clay, pounded fine and mixed with
linseed oil, will draw a boil to a head.*

SWEET PICKLED PEACHES

If you ain't got the right sort of peaches, crabapples will go fine.

RECIPE

3 pound peaches	2 ounces stick cinnamon
4 cups sugar	1 ounce whole cloves
1 pint vinegar	½ ounce whole ginger
1 cup water	

Blanch peaches 1 minute in boiling water. Plunge into cold water to cool, then peel. Freestone peaches can be pickled whole or split to remove the seed.

Make syrup by boiling 2 cups sugar, the water, vinegar and spices (in bags) for 3 minutes. If peaches are halved, boil 1 minute. Add remainder and cook until tender but not mushy. Cover and llet stand for a day. Drain off syrup and reheat. Pack in hot, sterile jars. Cover with hot syrup. Process pints 15 minutes below boiling (188). Then seal.

Pears and large apples can be pickled in same manner. If using crabapples or small pears, do not peel. Follow same recipe as above.

★　　★　　★

DILL PICKLES

2 quarts water	1 cup salt
1 quart vinegar	Boil, then cool
1 cup sugar	

Pack 6 quart pickles in jars after they have been crisped in cold water. Fill each jar with vinegar mixture. Also, add a large dill bunch in each jar. Don't seal tight until the third day.

★　　★　　★

ABOUT USIN CROCKS

Funny thing, but an old fashioned crock can give preserves a winey flavor you shore can't git out of glasses or jars. Marmalades in particular were Grandmaw's favorites, put up in crocks with sealing wax.

45

WATERMELON PICKLE

Like watermelon preserves, these are mighty good.

RECIPE

Skin and remove red meat from rind, then cut into pieces till you have six or seven pounds. Crisp in lime water, 1 cup lime for 2 gallons water. Soak 12 hours. Wash and boil until tender.

For syrup, take 4 pounds sugar, cover with water and start cooking. Add 1 quart vinegar, 2 tablespoons cinnamon bark, 1 tablespoon cloves and 1 tablespoon allspice when boiling starts. Cook 15 to 20 minutes. Store in crock or earthen jar for best results.

★　　★　　★

TOMATO JAM

4½ pounds ripe tomatoes   1½ cups vinegar
  peeled   ½ teaspoon allspice
4½ cups sugar   1 teaspoon cloves
1 tablespoon broken cinnamon

Scald and peel tomatoes, and then quarter them. Place in cooking pan and add sugar, vinegar, and spices. Cook slowly till thickened and then put in jars.

★　　★　　★

AUNT LIZA'S RHUBARB MARMALADE

You get a little bit tarter flavor than apples, but it's mighty good.

RECIPE

1 lemon   1 pound seedless raisins
2 oranges   3 pound sugar
4 pounds rhubarb

Remove juice from lemon and oranges and combine with the rhubarb cut into small pieces. Chop lemon and orange rind along with raisins. Add to the rhubarb. Mix all and let stand for 30 minutes. Add sugar and bring to a boil, then simmer one hour, stirring often. When the mixture gets thick, pour into glasses or crock. When cool, seal.

PEACH PRESERVES

Here's one time you can use the kernels

RECIPE

5 pounds peeled peaches in
halves or thick slices
3½ pounds sugar

3 pints water
5 peach kernels

Boil sugar and water until sugar dissolves. Add peaches and kernels. Cook till fruit is tender. Put in syrup while mixture is cooling. Process 20 minutes at simmering, then seal.

★　　★　　★

KRAUT

We'uns put a lot of stock in puttin up kraut and pickled stuff. Foller this recipe and you won't have trouble.

RECIPE

5 pounds cabbage
10 teaspoons salt

1 pound fills 1 pint jar

Clean old leaves off cabbage head (or heads). Quarter and slice off core. Shred cabbage. Put 5 pounds cabbage and salt in large pan and mix with hands. Pack into crock with potato masher. Pack gently. When crock is nearly full cover with cloth, plate and weight. It takes 6 to 8 days to ferment in summer weather. If it's cooler, it might take up to 12 days. Check daily and remove scum from top. Scald and wash the cloth to get rid of scum. When kraut is sour enough, you can leave it in crock and seal it with paraffin wax. Or, kraut can be sealed in sterilized glass jars, adding enough brine to fill the jar. Process 15 minutes below boiling point. Seal.

★　　★　　★

Ever want to dry herbs for winter use? Keep leaves on fresh cut herb. Cut stalks short. Put in uncovered jars with the leaves down. Dry in barely warm oven. Now you can seal in jars.

CHILI SAUCE

This is one sauce that can go with meat, fish, vegetables and even gravies.

RECIPE

5 quarts chopped ripe tomatoes

2 cups chopped red pepper

1½ cups chopped onion

3 tablespoons salt

1 cup sugar

3 cups vinegar

1 teaspoon cloves

1 teaspoon allspice

1 teaspoon cinnamon

Combine chopped vegetables, salt and sugar. Simmer until mix starts to thicken. Then add vinegar and spices and cook down till it becomes a thick sauce. Pour into hot, sterlized jars below boiling point (160) for 15 minutes. This makes three quarts.

★　　★　　★

PICKLED BEETS

Best results ain't from giant sized beets. Just kind of moderate in size. Boil and peel the beets first thing off.

RECIPE

Cut prepared beets as desired, or leave whole

1 pint sharp vinegar

2 tablespoons brown sugar

½ teaspoon salt

Green pepper (1 large)

⅛ teaspoon pepper

⅛ teaspoon paprika

2 cloves

Bring vinegar to boiling point, add sugar and seasonings. Arrange boiled beets in jar, alternating with bits of green pepper. Pour the boiling liquid over the beets. Then seal.

★　　★　　★

Madstones are shore hard to find, but they'll draw the poison from a mad dog's bite.

48

DIXIE RELISH

You put a heap of things into this recipe, but you also get a lot of good eatin, too.

RECIPE

1 quart chopped cabbage
1 pint chopped white onions
1 pint chopped sweet red
 pepper
1 pint chopped sweet green
 pepper
¾ cup sugar

4 tablespoons salt
4 tablespoons white mustard
 seed
2 tablespoons crushed celery
 seed.
1 quart cider vinegar

Salt peppers in brine (1 cup salt to 1 gallon water), for 24 hours. Freshen in cold water 1 or two hours. Drain. Remove seeds and coarse white sections. Chop separately and measure the chopped cabbage, peppers and onions before mixing. Add spices, sugar and vinegar. Let stand in crock or pan over night.

When ready to pack, drain vinegar off relish so that jars can be well packed. Pack in relish, pressing carefully. Then pour over it vinegar already drained off. Use wooden spatula to work out bubbles of air. Garnish each jar with 2 quarter-inch strips of red pepper 3 inches long. Place these strips vertically on opposite sides of jar interior. Adjust cap and process for 10 minutes at boiling point.

★ ★ ★

Blacksmith shops were in every community in horse and buggy days. There'd be wagons and buggies, with teams unhitched, menfolks talkin, kids scufflin and blacksmith poundin white hot iron on an anvil while his helper was shoein a horse, bent over with a hoof between his knees. Us young-uns liked to pull the forge's bellows handle, but not till after we learnt how.

SALETS

STUFFED CABBAGE

If you sort of git tired of regular boiled cabbage, try this.

1 pound chopped raw beef	1 teaspoon salt
½ pound chopped shoulder of pork.	½ teaspoon pepper
	1 medium size cabbage
1 good sized minced onion	Melted butter
½ cup flour	

Stir all ingredients before using the cabbage. Then break apart about a dozen cabbage leaves, scald and drain them. Put on each one and one half tablespoons of the mixture and fasten with a toothpick. Place in a saucepan, half cover with boiling water, add a little salt and cook about 35 minutes, with slow heat. Remove the toothpicks and serve with melted butter or cream gravy.

★   ★   ★

HOT TATER SALAD

6 medium potatoes	4 slices bacon, fried crisp
2 tablespoons chopped parsley	4 tablespoons salad oil
	½ tablespoon lemon juice
½ cup diced celery	Salt and pepper to taste
4 tablespoons vinegar	

Cook potatoes with jackets on in salt water. Cool, peel into slices or hunks. Break up bacon. Mix up vinegar, salad oil and lemon juice and heat just to boiling point. Pour half on potatoes, then add bacon, mixing it into potatoes. If you like, save some of celery with the parsley, to dress on top.

★   ★   ★

If lightnin has struck a tree down, don't use it for stovewood. It'll cause trubble, shore as you're born.

CONFEDERATE SLAW

We don't know exactly how this side dish got its name, unless the Daughters of the Confederacy gave it a title. The slaw is older 'n the Civil War, I reckon 'cause it's so downright good.

RECIPE

Shred one cabbage. Chop one red and one green pepper to one cabbage head. Keep cool till you add the other ingredients, that make up the dressing. Here it is:

3 tablespoons sugar   1 tablespoon flour
1 teaspoon salt

Mix this then add — 3 beaten eggs, 1 cup sweet milk. Cook in double boiler and pour in real slow a cup of vinegar as the mixture cooks. When dressing thickens, add 2 tablespoons butter and ½ teaspoon celery seed or celery salt. Take out of boiler and cool. Pour on cabbage and peppers.

★   ★   ★

WEATHER SIGNS

Git ready for a sudden cold wave when sows start bringin in mouths full of leaves and such to make warmer beds.

Never worry about red skies at dark. If it's red when you git up, watch out.

Spider's webs in the garden are thicker if early fall is comin.

A raincrow hollers a day ahead of bad weather, but if a peacock squawks it'll rain afore mornin.

Bees make good weather prophets. When they come stormin back to their hives in a hurry to git inside, take in the washin and dried apples and peaches.

DRINKS, CORDIALS AND TONICS

My grandpappy used to take a grubbin hoe and cut off sassafras roots, them that was plumb red and big. Grandmaw would take small pieces, soak them the night before, and cook up a batch, 'specially in the spring.

★　　★　　★

SASSAFRAS TEA

Take a handful of bits of root for every half gallon tea. Boil as you would coffee. If you like strong flavor, boil till the water turns darkish red. You can sweeten as you like. Don't throw the roots away. They'll last for several makings.

★　　★　　★

BLACKBERRY ROOT CORDIAL

It's good for dysentery.

To make a half gallon, use a handfull of blackberry knobs — or roots — which have been well washed. Boil for a half hour. Cool and put in a tablespoon cinnamon, a tablespoon cloves or allspice, a half cup sugar and, if you can git hold of any, one-fourth cup of grain alcohol.

★　　★　　★

RHUBARB

Folk naturally think of rhubarb cooked up several ways. Rhubarb powder got to be used a long time ago fur stomach troubles. Mixed with a little alcohol or wine, sugar syrup and sometimes a dab of baking soda, rhubarb cordial was a standby fur years and years, and now it can be store bought.

★　　★　　★

Stone bruises was the big worry when you turned out barefoot. Dew poisin was another.

CIDER

Cider presses and even big sausage mills can turn out a lot of apple cider. Mostly, if a person has enough trees, he's prepared to make cider, a lot of times on shares. Cider gits hard, and finally makes vinegar if it ain't strained and let boil a few minutes. The trick in making cider and not just apple juice, ain't well known to town folks. So, they miss a lot. Here's spicy, hot cider:

MULLED CIDER

1 gallon cider
¼ cup honey (Some use
  ½ cup brown sugar)

1 tablespoon ground
  cinnamon
1 tablespoon lemon juice
2 tablespoons cloves

Set on stove to simmer twenty minutes. Serve hot.

★   ★   ★

OTHER FRUIT JUICES

This takes in strawberries, cherries, raspberries, blackberries, elderberries, that can be covered with water and cooked just below boiling point for a half hour. Strain through double thickness of cheesecloth. If you want this as a smooth drink, add one cup of sugar to the gallon of juice.

WARNING! Don't add raisins and yeast and drain off through a waxed stopper by a tube. That might make wine! And it might blow up things.

★   ★   ★

PORE FOLKS COFFEE

When coffee run short back in Civil War days, a lot of folks, including Johnny Rebs, fixed up this sort of drink.

Hull out a handful small acorns, One handfull cracked wheat.

Roast. Pound in mortar. Boil and add sweetening, like honey.

53

WASSAIL DRINK

They brung this over from England, when we-uns lived in what they called The Colonies. This here drink is pronounced "(Wass-sul)" in spite of its spellin.

RECIPE

1 gallon sweet cider	2 sticks cinnamon
Juice of two oranges	1 teaspoon allspice
and 2 lemons	Half gallon water.
1 cup sugar	

After squeezing oranges and lemons, put rinds in 1 cup sugar, the cinnamon and allspice, and pour in half gallon water. Simmer for 30 minutes, then strain and cool. Now add juice of oranges and lemons and the cider. This recipe will serve 4 dozen persons. Serve hot.

★　　★　　★

HOT SPICED TEA

There's different opinions on the proper strength of tea but the following proportions should make enough tea for 16 servings, allowing ¾ cup to each one.

Pour 12 cups (three quarts) of boiling water over three tablespoons tea leaves, three two-inch sticks of cinnamon and about 1½ teaspoons whole cloves. Let steep for five minutes, strain and add one cup of sugar, 1/3 cup lemon juice and ¾ cup orange juice. Serve hot.

★　　★　　★

For lastin good smellin, nothin beats an apple stuck as full of cloves as a pin cushion. Wimmen would take a purty red apple, punch little holes in the skin and stick as many cloves as they could into the fruit. Then they'd hang it up in the front room, or bedroom. Some kept these clove apples in dressers and chests. I knowed one they claim was thirty-forty years old. The apple fruit was still firm.

CANDIES AND FROSTINS

MOLASSES CANDY

I reckon a candy pullin in the fall and winter git togeth-er was as much fun as anything.

RECIPE

1½ cup sorghum molasses   Stick of butter
½ cup sugar   Pinch of soda

Put sugar and molasses in sauce pan. Add ½ cup water Stir till dissolved. Cook till hairs string when you test with a spoon or fork. Now add a stick of butter and stir. Pour into bowl which has been buttered or greased. Grease hands well and pick up product when it's cool enough to stand it. Now this kind, you don't have to pull but a few times, till you get a golden look. Pour on plates, let spread, then cut into squares to cool.

★   ★   ★

CRYSTALIZED PEELS AND FRUITS

You can fix up orange and lemon peel, grapefruit rind, watermelon rind and figs this way. Fine for a fruit cake.

RECIPE

Take a fine grater and break oil cells in rinds like orange and grapefruit, then cut into pieces. Cover with cold water and parboil 5 or 6 times, beginning with cold water each time. Cook till tender. Drain, cook equal weights of fruit, sugar and water, to 220 degrees. If you like coloring, add 6 drops coloring to the pound of fruit before cooking first time. Let stand 24 hours. Finish at 228 degrees till fruit is tender all the way through. Lift from hot syrup and put on trays to dry. When no longer sticky, roll in granulated sugar and store. Other fruits mentioned can be crystalized the same way.

FONDANTS

This can be made raw or cooked.

★ ★ ★

COOKED FONDANT

1 cup water   2½ cups sugar
⅛ teaspoon cream of tartar. Dissolve in pan.

Boil to soft ball stage, 238 degrees F. for soft fondant. 242 F. for hard fondant) To prevent crystalizing, boil with lid on. Pour on greased platters and cool enough to be handled. Beat with two knives till creamy, then knead with the hands till foundant is soft and velvety. Keep in jar. To use, melt in double over hot water. If you want to flavor this, put it in at first boiling stage.

★ ★ ★

RAW FONDANT

Cream ¼ pound of butter. Add enough powdered sugar to make fondant stiff enough to handle. Mould to any shape desired. Color and flavor as desired.

★ ★ ★

MOLASSES CIRCLES

You got hungry young uns around, keep these handy.

RECIPE

1 cup shortening	3 cups sifted flour
½ cup molasses	1 teaspoon cinnamon
1 cup sugar	1 teaspoon ginger
1 egg	½ teaspoon mace
¾ teaspoon vinegar	2 teaspoons bakng soda
¾ cup rich milk or	1 teaspoon salt
light cream	

Cream shortening and sugar. Add well beaten egg. Add molasses and beat well. Combine vinegar and milk. Sift flour, spices, baking soda and salt. Add alternately with milk mixture. Drop by tablespoons about 2 inches apart on greased sheets. Bake in moderate oven (350) 8 to 10 minutes. Should make six dozen.